JUN 2 4 2012

Lexile:

LSU ☑yes
SJB ☐yes
BL: 4.7
Pts: 1.0

VELOCITY™

THE MOST Disgusting
Jobs ON THE PLANET

BY JOHN PERRITANO

CAPSTONE PRESS
a capstone imprint

Velocity is published by Capstone Press,
1710 Roe Crest Drive, North Mankato, Minnesota 56003.
www.capstonepub.com

Books published by Capstone Press are manufactured with paper
containing at least 10 percent post-consumer waste.

Library of Congress Cataloging-in-Publication Data

Perritano, John.
  The most disgusting jobs on the planet /by John Perritano.
    p. cm.—(Velocity. Disgusting stuff)
  Includes bibliographical references and index.
  Summary: "Discusses some of the most vile, gross jobs from around the world"—Provided
by publisher.
  ISBN 978-1-4296-7532-1 (library binding)
  1. Occupations—Juvenile literature.
  2. Vocational guidance—Juvenile literature. I. Title. II. Series.
  HF5381.2.P43 2012
    331.702—dc23   2011029193

Editor: Barbara Linde
Project Manager: Archna Bisht
Art Director: Suzan Kadribasic
Designer: Ankita Sharma, Manish Kumar
Image Researchers: Akansha Srivastava, Saloni Vaid

Photo Credits
Alamy: Imagebroker, 42-43, Maximilian Weinzierl, 45 (top); AP Images: Toby Talbot/Associated Press,
20-21, AL Grillo/Associated Press, 22-23; Corbis: Bettmann, 32 (top), Ted Soqui, 36-37; Fotolia: Saidin
B Jusoh, 28; iStockphoto: Seraficus, 8-9, Beerkoff, 35 (top), Lopshire Photography, 36 (center); Max
Planck Institute For Evolutionary/Frank Vinken, 16-17; Photolibrary: Uwe Moser/Picture Press, Cover,
Guy Moberly/Fresh Food Images, title, Michel Gunther, 6-7, Guy Moberly/Fresh Food Images, 38;
Reuters: Sukree Sukplang, 4-5, Stringer Shanghai, 24-25, Sean Yong, 26-27, Nicky Loh, 44-45; Science
Photo Library: Biomedical Imaging Unit,Southampton general hospital, 13, David Parker, 18-19, Steve
Gschmeissner, 29, Ria Novosti, 34-35, DR Morley Read, 40-41; Shutterstock: Jo Crebbin, 10-11, Leonello
Calvetti, 12, Artem Rudik, 14, Simon Krzic, 15, keriatti, 23 (bottom), Bogdan Ionescu, 24 (bottom),
Psamtik, 27 (top), Fedorov Oleksiy, 28-29, David Ryznar, 30-31, Selyutina Olga, 32-33, Deepspacedave,
34-35 (top), Vladimir Koletic, 43; Thinkstock: iStockphoto, 8 (top), Hemera, 31 (top).

Printed in the United States of America in Stevens Point, Wisconsin.
102011   006404WZS12

Table of Contents

It's a Dirty Job!

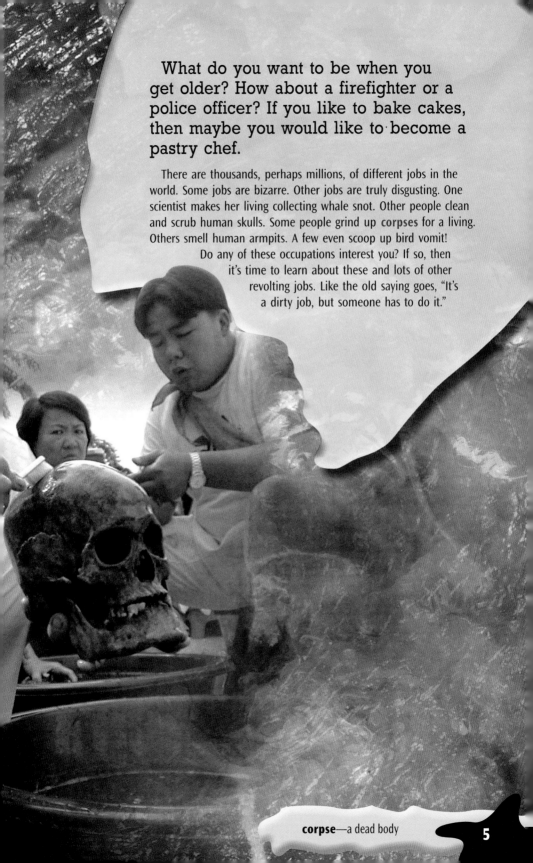

What do you want to be when you get older? How about a firefighter or a police officer? If you like to bake cakes, then maybe you would like to become a pastry chef.

There are thousands, perhaps millions, of different jobs in the world. Some jobs are bizarre. Other jobs are truly disgusting. One scientist makes her living collecting whale snot. Other people clean and scrub human skulls. Some people grind up **corpses** for a living. Others smell human armpits. A few even scoop up bird vomit! Do any of these occupations interest you? If so, then it's time to learn about these and lots of other revolting jobs. Like the old saying goes, "It's a dirty job, but someone has to do it."

corpse—a dead body

Chapter 1
Pooper Scoopers

Sewer workers spend their days covered in poop. But they have a very important job. By cleaning poop, the workers help keep people healthy.

Sewer Rats

Did you ever wonder what happens when you flush the toilet? Where does your poop go? Where does the toilet paper go? Does it disappear?

No, your poop doesn't vanish. Most poop travels through a sewer system. Sewer systems are a series of pipes. Those pipes move dirty water from toilets and sinks to a sewer treatment plant.

Sewer workers make sure that the poop runs through the system smoothly. If they don't do their job, sewage can pollute the environment and make people sick.

One thing sewer workers do is clean your poop. How? Inside the sewer plants are large pools of poop and water. Plant workers put bacteria in the pools. The bacteria eat the organic matter in the water. Eventually clean sewer water is pumped back into rivers and streams.

Sewer workers also remove dirty diapers and other foul things that people flush down the pipes. They scoop up yards of hair that clog the sewer plant's machines. They shovel wet, muddy sludge created by human waste.

bacteria—very small living things that exist all around you and inside you; some bacteria cause disease
organic—produced by animals or plants

Sewer plants smell of feces and a gas called methane. Sewer workers smell of poop when they leave work. The workers get used to the stench. But they definitely can't stop at a restaurant on the way home!

Septic Warriors

Some homes are not connected to a sewer system. These homes use underground septic tanks. Septic tanks are mini-sewer plants. Bacteria in the tank cause poop and other waste to decompose, or break down. What doesn't decay settles to the bottom. What happens when the tank is full? A septic pumper vacuums out the sludge.

Porta-Putrid

Porta-potties are portable toilets. Rows of these modern outhouses are often set up at county fairs, construction sites, and public parks.

urinal

ventilation pipe

Only one person at a time can use a porta-potty. There are no pipes or running water. There's just a seat with a hole in the middle. When people use a porta-potty, their waste splashes into a pot of chemicals. These chemicals disinfect and deodorize the poop and pee.

Porta-potty cleaners wear eye protection and gloves to shield themselves from germs. They don't want to get feces on their hands or in their eyes. If they do, they might get sick.

Cleaning the portable toilets is not easy. Porta-potty cleaners clean up wads of used toilet paper. Then they spray the inside with a cleaning solution. The liquid dissolves the dirt and grime. The spray also kills bacteria.

Finally, the cleaners vacuum up the human waste and chemicals from inside the porta-potty toilet. Cleaners replace the chemicals so the porta-potty will be ready to be sent to the next event.

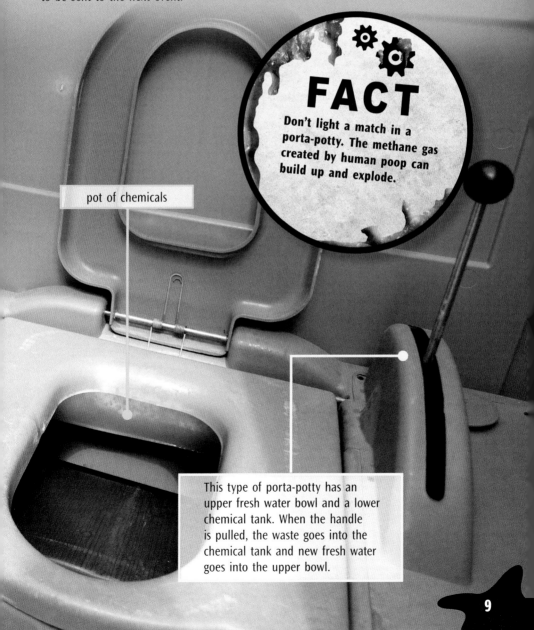

FACT

Don't light a match in a porta-potty. The methane gas created by human poop can build up and explode.

pot of chemicals

This type of porta-potty has an upper fresh water bowl and a lower chemical tank. When the handle is pulled, the waste goes into the chemical tank and new fresh water goes into the upper bowl.

Chapter 2

Gross Science

Some scientists don't mind getting dirty. They study some pretty disgusting things! Still, scientists have important work to do. What they learn can help people live better lives.

Hot for Snot

Dr. Karina Acevedo-Whitehouse is a zoologist. But the wild animals she studies do not live in a zoo. And her job does not involve giving shots or taking temperatures. Her patients live in the ocean. And her job is to collect whale snot.

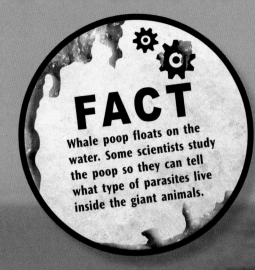

Whales are big, but the ocean is even bigger. It is difficult to keep track of whales to see if they are healthy. That's why Karina found a way to collect whale snot. When a whale comes up for air, a mixture of air and water, called blow, shoots out of the whale's blow hole. If the whale is sick, snot will shoot out as well. Karina collects samples of the blow to see if the whale is sick.

Karina uses a remote-controlled helicopter to catch the snot. The helicopter looks like a toy, but it is actually much more important than that. Attached to the bottom is a special dish. Karina flies the helicopter near the whale. Suddenly, thar she blows! The snot shoots out of the blowhole and sticks to the dish.

When the helicopter lands, Karina puts the samples under a microscope. She looks for bacteria, fungi, and anything else that can make a whale sick. Karina studies whales and their health to make sure that they don't become extinct, or die out.

fungi—organisms that have no leaves, flowers, or roots; mushrooms and molds are fungi

Poo Player

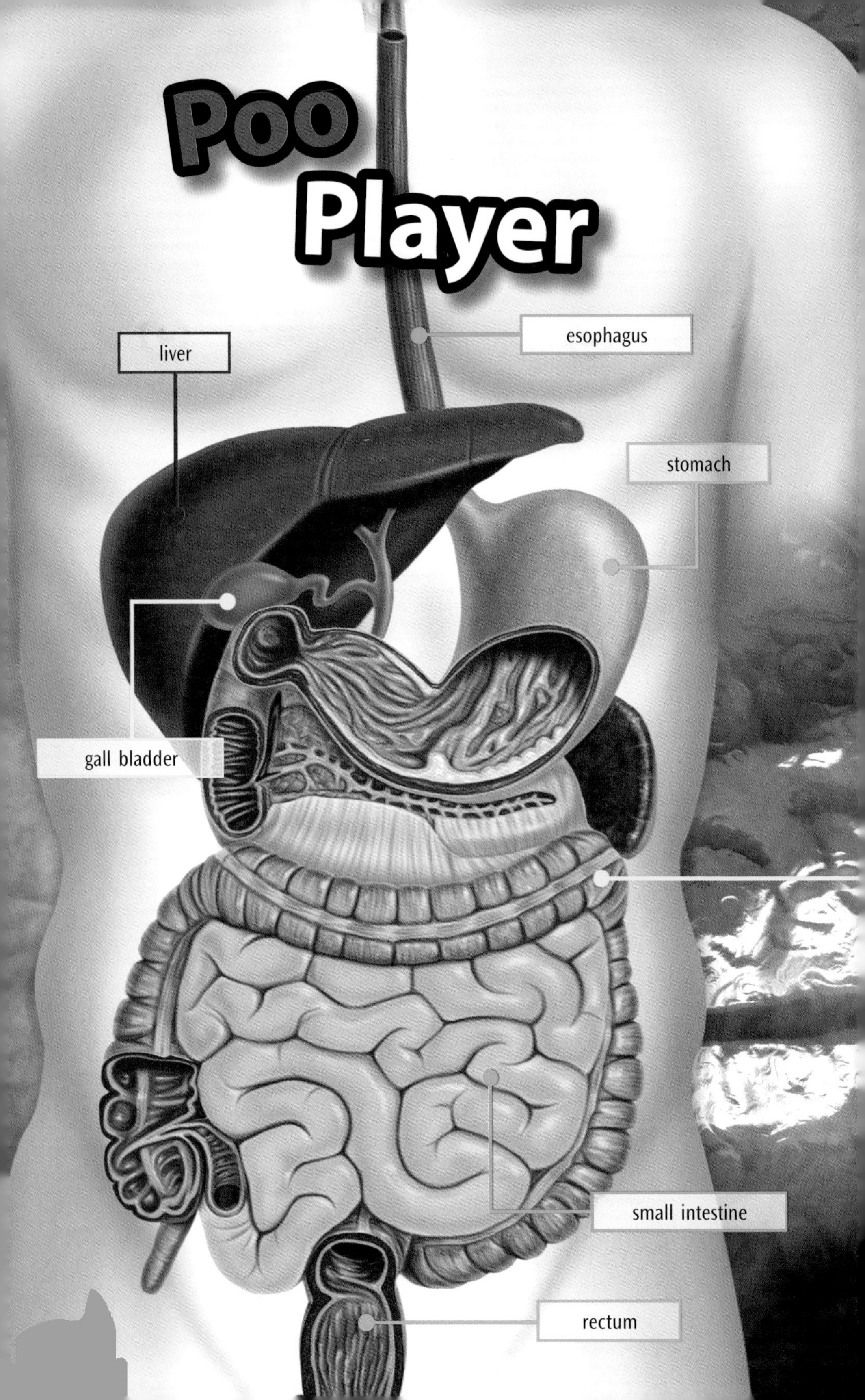

esophagus

liver

stomach

gall bladder

small intestine

rectum

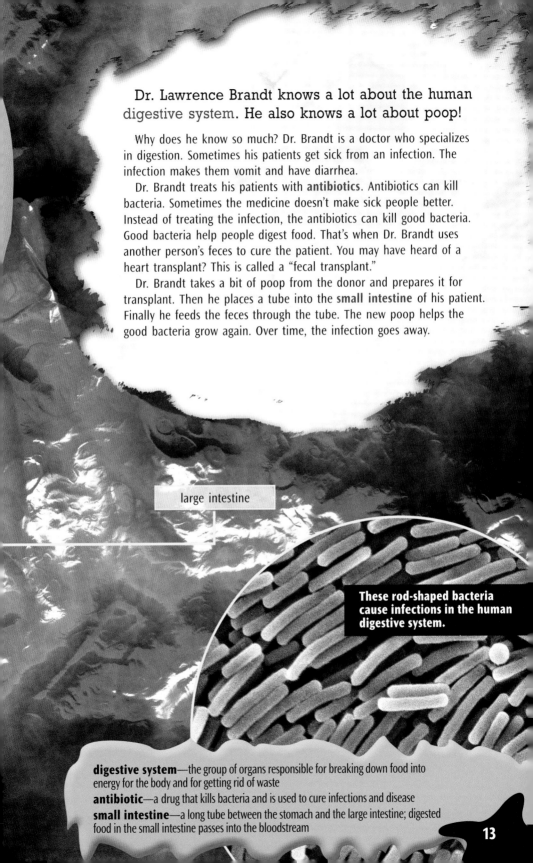

Dr. Lawrence Brandt knows a lot about the human digestive system. He also knows a lot about poop!

Why does he know so much? Dr. Brandt is a doctor who specializes in digestion. Sometimes his patients get sick from an infection. The infection makes them vomit and have diarrhea.

Dr. Brandt treats his patients with **antibiotics**. Antibiotics can kill bacteria. Sometimes the medicine doesn't make sick people better. Instead of treating the infection, the antibiotics can kill good bacteria. Good bacteria help people digest food. That's when Dr. Brandt uses another person's feces to cure the patient. You may have heard of a heart transplant? This is called a "fecal transplant."

Dr. Brandt takes a bit of poop from the donor and prepares it for transplant. Then he places a tube into the **small intestine** of his patient. Finally he feeds the feces through the tube. The new poop helps the good bacteria grow again. Over time, the infection goes away.

large intestine

These rod-shaped bacteria cause infections in the human digestive system.

digestive system—the group of organs responsible for breaking down food into energy for the body and for getting rid of waste

antibiotic—a drug that kills bacteria and is used to cure infections and disease

small intestine—a long tube between the stomach and the large intestine; digested food in the small intestine passes into the bloodstream

Ouch!

Mosquitoes have been buzzing for 30 million years. They can carry many diseases, including **malaria**. Scientist Helge Zieler used to have a crazy job. Helge studied mosquitoes to learn how the insects spread disease.

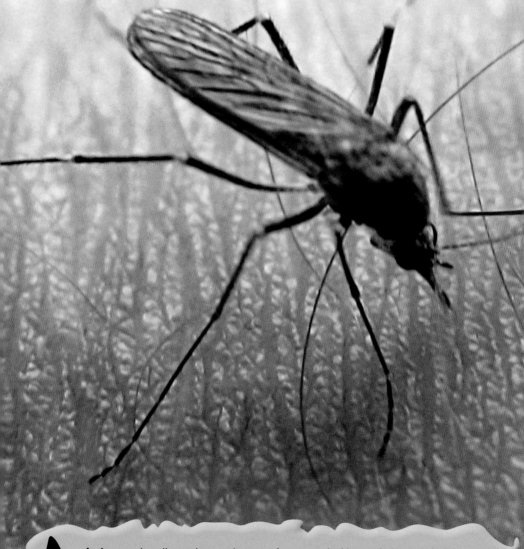

malaria—a serious disease that people can get from mosquito bites; malaria causes high fever, chills, and sometimes death

FACT

The red bump and itching you get from a mosquito bite is actually an allergic reaction to the mosquito's saliva.

What was the crazy part of his job? Since it's not easy to catch a mosquito, Helge used himself as bait! Helge found a nice buggy area for his work. He sat inside a mosquito net with a hole in the bottom. The mosquitoes took notice. They were attracted by the warmth of Helge's body.

Within minutes, mosquitoes started flying through the hole in the net. Helge wore short pants. *Buzzzzzzzzzzzz!* The mosquitoes quickly took aim and dove on Helge's bare legs.

When a mosquito landed, Helge placed a straw-like tube over the bug. He sucked the insect into the tube with his mouth. Once he captured the insect, Helge exhaled. The bug fell out of the tube and into a container. On his best day, Helge caught 500 mosquitoes (and got 3,000 bites) in three hours!

Chapter 3
Body Shop

Some people throw their entire bodies into their work. Others use the heads and bones of others.

Bone Crusher

Meat grinders. Cheese grinders. Coffee grinders. People grind up many things—including dead bodies!

Grinding the bones of a dead person is the job of a corpse grinder. Corpse grinders are forensic scientists. Forensic scientists study evidence when a crime has been committed.

When police investigate, they might find bones buried in a field or a corpse in a basement. When such things happen, police want to know who the bones belong to, and how that person died. They call in a corpse grinder to help them.

Corpse grinders take bits of bone and grind them into powder. They are then able to remove **DNA** from the powder. DNA is a type of molecule found in the body's cells. Every person's DNA is unique.

The corpse grinders study the DNA. They can identify someone by comparing the corpse's DNA with the DNA of people believed to be relatives.

Scientists used this identification process after terrorists flew two planes into the World Trade Center in New York City on September 11, 2001. Scientists were then able to discover the identity of many World Trade Center victims.

DNA—material in cells that gives people their individual characteristics

Doctor to the Dead

From surgeons to pediatricians, there are many types of doctors. There are also doctors who study dead people. These doctors are called medical examiners.

Medical examiners perform autopsies, which are special operations. These operations can help determine how and when a person died. Autopsies can take hours to perform.

Medical examiners first look at the outside of the body. They look for any injury that might have caused the person to die.

They then inspect the corpse's organs. They put small slices of these organs under a microscope. By looking through the microscope, the medical examiners can see the body's cells. By studying the cells, the medical examiners can often tell if the person died from a disease, drug overdose, or some other reason.

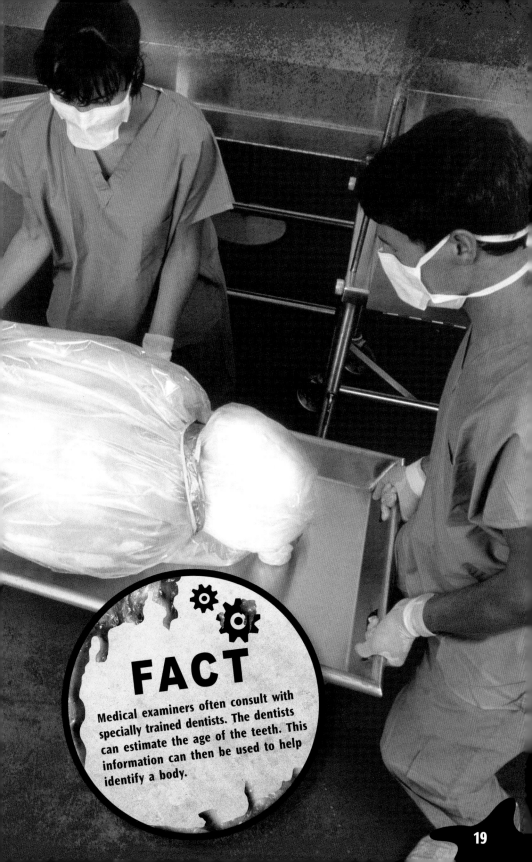

You
Smell !

Wanted: Person with a good sense of smell. Applicant should not be afraid of getting close to people and should enjoy smelling armpits.

Have you ever wondered why underarm deodorant smells nice? Or why fresh cat litter has a pleasing scent? How do people know whether disposable diapers can mask the smell of a baby's poop?

It's the job of an odor judge to help companies figure out whether a product does what it is supposed to do. Some judges work for mouthwash companies. They let people with bad breath breathe in their faces. That's the only way to tell whether a mouthwash works. Odor judges also work for deodorant companies. They put their noses under people's armpits to test the products. Take a whiff! Perfume companies hire odor judges too. They want to make sure their fragrances smell nice.

One odor judge's job was to sniff space shuttles. For 30 years, George Aldrich worked for NASA, the space agency of the United States. His job was to smell everything in the space shuttles. Why? Astronauts can get sick in space if something smells bad. If astronauts are sick, they might not be able to do their jobs. If they can't do their jobs, they can put the spacecraft and mission in danger.

Gas Pass

Everyone passes gas. You pass gas at least 10 times a day. One doctor in Minnesota believes that smelling flatulence can tell a lot about a person's health. Michael Levitt, the doctor who studies farts, says flatulence that smells really bad could be a sign of a disease in a person's stomach or intestines.

He paid several people to smell farts. He used a tube to collect the gas in glass containers. The odor judges then opened the jars one at a time. They took a whiff, and then they rated how bad each fart smelled. The samples were also studied to see what types of gas were in each fart.

Thick Skulled

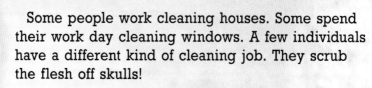

Some people work cleaning houses. Some spend their work day cleaning windows. A few individuals have a different kind of cleaning job. They scrub the flesh off skulls!

Buffalo skulls. Moose skulls. Bear skulls—even human skulls. You name it, some skulls just have to be cleaned. In fact, cleaning the flesh off these bones is big business. That's because teachers need clean skulls so their students can learn about animals. And medical students need clean human skulls to learn about human **anatomy**.

The first step in cleaning a skull is to scrub off most of its flesh. The cleaner then places the skull in boiling water. Once the boiling begins, the clear water quickly turns a putrid brown from the flesh left on the skull. A layer of oil from the boiling flesh and bone forms on top. After a while, the remaining flesh on the skull melts off. The skulls are then air-dried.

For another cleaning method, the bones are placed in a tub crawling with hundreds of beetles. The beetles chow down on the remaining flesh.

Using the beetles is a dirty, messy, smelly way of cleaning a skull. But the bugs do a good job. They eat every bit of meat. The beetles don't damage the bones as much as other cleaning methods. However, it does take the beetles several weeks to completely eat away all of the flesh.

anatomy—scientific study of the body and how its parts are arranged

Chapter 4

Freaky Farmers

Farms can be wonderful places. Animals live on farms. Farmers grow apples, corn, and wheat. But farms can also be pretty disgusting.

Flies in the Muck

All farms have flies. Some farms have more than others. Just ask Pam and Dennis Ponsness. They are farmers, but they don't tend to sheep, cows, or horses. They don't even grow corn. Instead, Pam and Dennis raise maggots, or baby flies.

Pam and Dennis sell maggots to scientists. The scientists use the maggots in research laboratories. The couple also sells maggots to doctors who use them to heal wounds. A doctor puts the maggots on an infected open cut. The maggots chew and dissolve dead tissue while killing bacteria. Then they swallow the bacteria that caused the infection. Pam and Dennis also sell the maggots to fishermen, who use the critters as bait. They sell 3 to 4 million maggots a week.

It's easy to start a maggot farm. All you need are bins, rotten meat, and flies. Flies are attracted to rotten food. The farmers put the meat in the bins. When flies land on rotting food, they vomit, which makes the food easier to eat.

When the flies are finished vomiting and eating, they lay eggs on the rotting meat. When the eggs hatch, maggots crawl out. The key is to harvest the maggots every day and keep them well fed.

Flies with Flair

Erin Watson is a scientist at Southeastern Louisiana University. She is also an art lover of the buggy kind. Her favorite artists are maggots. She gently places maggots into nontoxic paint and then onto a blank canvas. The maggots use their hook-like mouths to crawl across the canvas. As they move, they drag rivers of paint behind them. She shows off the maggot artwork to help get kids interested in science.

Keep
Off!

Freeze-dried Urine

Animal pee remains fresh for 90 days. Freeze-dried urine lasts longer. People freeze-dry urine the same way they freeze-dry food. The liquid urine goes through a special machine. The machine freezes the pee, allowing the water to evaporate. That turns the liquid pee into a solid. The solid is packaged as a powder and sold. When a person buys freeze-dried pee, all they have to do is add water. The powdered pee turns to liquid again.

The squirrels are eating the tulip bulbs. The rabbits are nibbling holes in the cabbage. What's a gardener to do?

They can go to the store and buy the urine of a large **predator**. The urine comes in a bottle. One whiff and the rabbit or squirrel runs away. Why? The tiny critters smell the pee and think a larger animal is lurking.

Gardeners aren't the only people who use animal urine. Hunters buy female deer urine. Hunters spray the urine around the forest. They use it to attract male deer. Hunters spend $70 million a year on deer urine!

How is animal urine collected? Urine farmers raise animals, such as deer, on their farm. They leave water in a barn for the animals to drink. The animals pee. Their urine flows though grates in the barn's floor. Under these grates is a second floor. This one is V-shaped. The animal pee hits that floor. The urine runs down into a big tub. When the vat is filled, workers store the urine in a refrigerator. They then bottle and sell the animal pee.

Pig urine can be used as an ingredient in organic fertilizer.

Chapter 5
Animal Harvesters

Round-up time for these animals can be a truly revolting experience.

Spit and Heal

Today's doctors use leeches to help restore blood circulation in patients who have had a finger or toe sewn back on. How does a leech do this job? First, a leech attaches its mouth to the skin of the patient. It then begins to feed. The saliva in the leech's mouth expands the blood vessels between the once-severed veins in the toe or finger. Blood can then flow freely again. In addition, the leech's spit acts as a pain killer.

Bloodsuckers

Centuries ago, the local barber was often also the local doctor. People believed that bloodsucking leeches could cure a person of an illness. Most of the time, the leeches just made the problem worse.

Today, people use leeches as fish bait. Leech collectors have the gross, but easy, job of trapping the leeches. Leeches look like fat worms with suckers on each end.

Their suckers will stick to just about anything. Some collectors use coffee cans as traps. Others use cloth sacks. Some make traps out of milk jugs. The best place to catch leeches is in ponds, lakes, and streams. Collectors need to be careful when removing the leeches from the trap, however. The animals can latch onto their fingers and hands. Most collectors use bits of bloody meat to attract the slimy creatures.

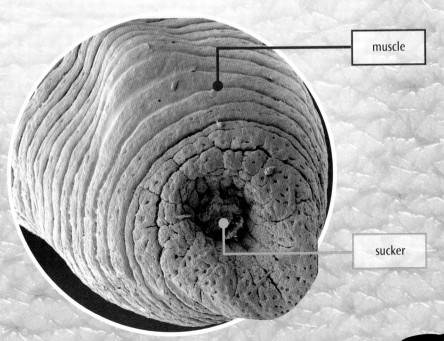

muscle

sucker

Using Your Noodle

Catfish are huge. Some have heads as big as basketballs. Catfish look scary, but they are good to eat. Most people catch catfish with a fishing rod. Others use their hands—and that's no fish story! It's a traditional way of catching fish, especially in the southern United States.

Bare-handed fishing goes by several names. The most popular is noodling. Others call it grabbing. Some call it hogging. How does a noodler noodle? Catfish hang out under rocks and near logs. To find the fish, noodlers wade along a riverbank. They search the water with their hands.

Some noodlers will use dead fish that have been rotting over time to attract catfish. Bacteria eat the flesh of the fish, turning it into a gooey mess. Noodlers wipe their arms with these stinky fish guts.

Noodlers also need to be careful. They can accidentally grab onto a beaver or a snapping turtle. Chomp!

Expert noodlers grab the fish by its mouth or gills. Once the fish is snagged, the noodlers wrap their legs around the catfish's tail and force it to the surface. That's not as easy as it sounds. Some catfish can weigh up to 50 pounds (23 kilograms).

Chapter 6
Rubbish Warriors

Each day an army of people pick up household trash and scrub crime scenes clean. Others risk their lives disposing of dangerous waste. Who are these rubbish warriors? Read on!

Take Out the Trash

Ronald Bell is a sanitation worker. Each morning he climbs aboard a truck and picks up other people's trash.

The truck has a large blade that squeezes the trash. Sometimes the bags burst. If Ronald doesn't get out of the way, he gets sprayed with rotten food, old milk, and used cat litter.

Most people take sanitation workers for granted. Every day the workers live with the smell of putrid garbage. They battle maggots, roaches, and other bugs that buzz around rotting meat and vegetables. They step in water that seeps out of the garbage bags.

If the workers aren't careful, they could get very sick. People throw all sorts of things away, including chemicals and human and animal waste. Garbage bags can be brimming with bacteria and poisonous liquids that can cause illness.

Fluid Fighters

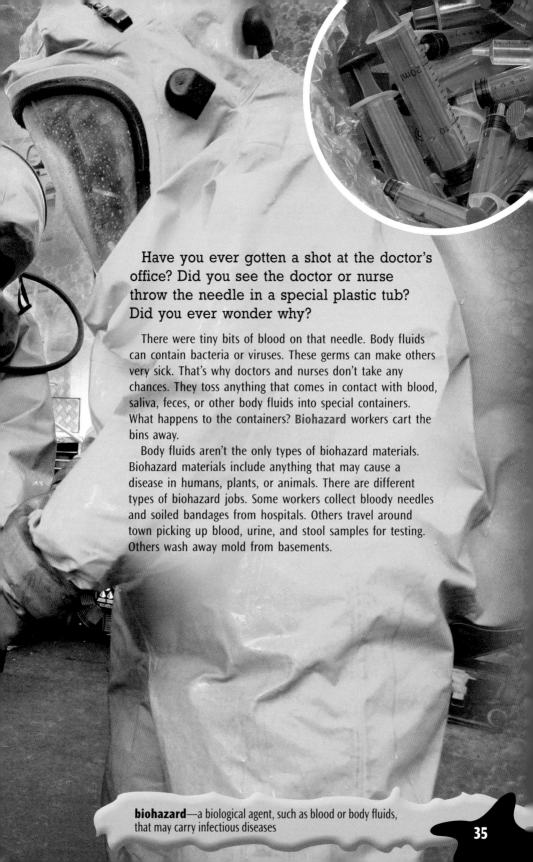

Have you ever gotten a shot at the doctor's office? Did you see the doctor or nurse throw the needle in a special plastic tub? Did you ever wonder why?

There were tiny bits of blood on that needle. Body fluids can contain bacteria or viruses. These germs can make others very sick. That's why doctors and nurses don't take any chances. They toss anything that comes in contact with blood, saliva, feces, or other body fluids into special containers. What happens to the containers? **Biohazard** workers cart the bins away.

Body fluids aren't the only types of biohazard materials. Biohazard materials include anything that may cause a disease in humans, plants, or animals. There are different types of biohazard jobs. Some workers collect bloody needles and soiled bandages from hospitals. Others travel around town picking up blood, urine, and stool samples for testing. Others wash away mold from basements.

biohazard—a biological agent, such as blood or body fluids, that may carry infectious diseases

Blood Scrubbers

When the police leave the scene of a crime, there can often be a big mess to clean up.

Many times a victim's family has to put things back in order. But crime scenes can't simply be dusted and vacuumed. Special cleaning crews need to do the work. Crime scenes are often full of blood and other biohazard materials. Crime scene cleaners use special fluids and equipment to scrub the area.

Every clean-up job is different. Sometimes workers have to rip out blood-soaked carpeting. Crime scene cleaners also use special machines to remove the odors left behind by decaying corpses.

Some crime scenes are contaminated with chemicals. The chemicals can make a crime scene cleaner sick. The chemicals can also explode if not handled properly.

Chapter 7

That ~~Stinks!~~ Stinks!

There's nothing worse than coming home from work smelly and dirty. But what do you expect if you handle dead animals all day?

Cooking Carcasses

Dead farm animals need to be disposed of quickly. A decaying animal can spread disease. So what do farmers do when an animal has died?

They send dead animals to rendering plants. Plant workers separate animal fat from the meat and bones. These products are then shipped to factories where they are used to make things like pet food, soaps, crayons, and lipstick.

Removing the hides of the dead animals is the first thing a rendering plant worker does. The animals are then fed into a big grinder. The grinder chews up the carcasses. It spits out a huge pile of bone and flesh. That pile is then shoveled into a high-temperature cooker.

As the animals' remains cook, workers separate the liquid fat from the bones. Workers then move the fat into individual tanks. Inside the tanks, the fat cools into lard.

rendering—the process of separating animal fat from meat by slowly heating it

Vulgar Vomit

What do you call a person who picks up owl vomit? An avian vomitologist, of course!

"Avian vomitologist" is a made-up name, but Don Cicoletti says it is the perfect description of his job. Owls swallow their food—generally mice—whole. Fluids in the owl's stomach digest the mouse meat. But there's a lot of stuff, such as bones and fur, that the owl can't digest. All this material gathers in the animal's gizzard.

The gizzard is a muscular pouch in the owl's digestive system. The gizzard works like a household trash compactor. It squeezes all the bones and fur into something that looks like a piece of charcoal. Eventually, the pellets get too large for the owl to handle. About 12 hours after its meal, the owl throws up the pellets.

Don's job is to search for these neat little balls of fur and bones. He packages them and sells them to schools. At the schools, students pry the vomit apart. They learn about owls and what they eat by studying the pellets.

Ewwwwww! No one wants to touch owl vomit, do they? It's OK. The pellets are **sterilized** before reaching the schools.

sterilize—to clean something so thoroughly that no germs or dirt remain

an opened barn owl pellet

Hook,
Line, and
Fish Heads

Imagine opening a can of tuna and seeing a pair of eyes staring back at you. Thanks to fish mongers and cannery workers, that doesn't happen.

Fish mongers and cannery workers slice, dice, and peel fresh fish. They work at fish markets preparing the fish for sale. Inside the cannery, dead fish are placed on a long conveyor belt, where they are sorted and washed.

Workers cut off the fish heads and tails. Then they slice open the bellies. They remove the insides. The conveyor belt is red with blood.

After they are gutted, the fish go down another conveyor belt. The fish are washed again, and then the flesh is prepared to be sold in packages and cans.

Where do the fish parts go?

In some canneries, the heads fall into bins. They are sometimes then used to make fish head soup, which is popular in Asia. Fish heads also make a great garden fertilizer. The fish guts and bones are thrown into another bin to make fish food. Fish scales can be crushed and used in lipstick.

Pest
Control

Each day, Rob Young prepares for war. He's not a soldier. He's an exterminator. He battles bees, bedbugs, rats, and cockroaches.

These pests make most people shudder. Not Rob. He doesn't faint in fright when he comes across a rat. He doesn't bat an eye when he sees a bat. Spring is Rob's busiest time of the year. That's when ants and other bugs begin marching into homes and buildings. They get into cracks and crawl up through the walls.

Exterminators like Rob deal with all types of pests. Some battle snakes lurking in backyards. Others look for bedbugs hiding under mattresses. Exterminators often squeeze themselves into small spaces where creepy crawlies lurk.

One exterminator in Peoria, Arizona, reported on the Internet that he found a house full of crickets. He had to step around piles of cricket droppings. When he took a hose and sprayed water around the home, hundreds of the bugs scampered for cover.

Reality TV show star "Billy the Exterminator" had to remove nearly 15,000 bees from a hive in a house. He carefully vacuumed the bees and took them to a bee keeper.

A Job for You?

Here's hoping you enjoyed this jaunt through some of the world's dirtiest jobs. But even though you may not want to think about it, there are many more! How many disgusting jobs can you name?

Glossary

anatomy (uh-NA-tuh-mee)—scientific study of the body and how its parts are arranged

antibiotic (an-ti-bye-OT-ik)—a drug that kills bacteria and is used to cure infections and disease

bacteria (bak-TEER-ee-uh)—very small living things that exist all around you and inside you; some bacteria cause disease

biohazard (BY-oh-ha-zuhrd)—a biological agent, such as blood or body fluids, that may carry infectious diseases

corpse (KORPS)—a dead body

digestive system (dye-JESS-tiv SISS-tuhm)—the group of organs responsible for breaking down food into energy for the body and for getting rid of waste

DNA (dee-en-AY)—material in cells that gives people their individual characteristics

fungi (FUHN-jy)—organisms that have no leaves, flowers, or roots; mushrooms and molds are fungi

malaria (muh-LAIR-ee-ah)—a serious disease that people get from mosquito bites; malaria causes high fever, chills, and sometimes death

organic (or-GAN-ik)—produced by animals or plants

predator (PRED-uh-tur)—an animal that hunts other animals for food

rendering (REN-dur-ing)—the process of separating animal fat from meat by slowly heating it

small intestine (SMAWL in-TESS-tin)—a long tube between the stomach and the large intestine; digested food in the small intestine passes into the bloodstream

sterilize (STER-uh-lize)—to clean something so thoroughly that no germs or dirt remain

Read More

King, Bart. *The Big Book of Gross Stuff.* Layton, Utah: Gibbs Smith, 2010.

Reeves, Diane Lindsey. *Gross Jobs.* New York: Ferguson, 2009.

Silverstein, Alvin, Virginia Silverstein, and Laura Silverstein Nunn. *Poop Collectors, Armpit Sniffers, and More: The Yucky Jobs Book.* Berkeley Heights, N.J.: Enslow Publishers, 2011.

Internet Sites

FactHound offers a safe, fun way to find Internet sites related to this book. All of the sites on FactHound have been researched by our staff.

Here's all you do:

Visit *www.facthound.com*

Type in this code: 9781429675321

Index